His Name Is
The Word

Pastor Kenneth Johnson

His Name Is The Word
Copyright © 2012 by Pastor Kenneth Johnson

Printed in USA by 48HrBooks (www.48HrBooks.com)

Table of Contents

Acknowledgements

I want to say thank you to my wife, who has been my biggest supporter and fan through the good times and the bad. I want to thank my kids for loving their father unconditionally, and to my mother and mother in-law for being two of the sweetest people in the world. I also want to thank my Aunt Wendy for always being there for me, and to my family and my church family, which are far too many to name. Thanks for being there for me. I love you all! I want to give a special thanks to Pastors Denorvice Howard, Pastor Lanell Caldwell, and Pastor Don Couch for being wonderful examples of how real men of God are supposed to look. Your example of being faithful pastors, husbands and fathers set a wonderful foundation for the life I now live. God bless you.

A special thanks goes out to my pastors the apostles, Mom and Dad Carter of Sanctuary Evangelistic Church in Tulsa, Oklahoma. Your wisdom, guidance, and love are amazing. You have been a rock to me in some very turbulent times, and for that I say thank you. To every pastor, minister, friend, and associate whom I didn't call by name— you're too numerous to name, and the impact you've made is too great to be contained in this one writing. However, I want to say thank you for every kind word, prayer, and thoughtful gesture. I love you from the depths of my soul, and the seeds you have planted in my life and ministry will be remembered forever.
To Damon James, my best friend forever, I just want to say thank you publicly for being my true friend. Your honesty and integrity have helped guide me in many critical moments in my life. I'll never forget your words of wisdom

when I thought I was the super saint who would never make a mistake again after being filled with the Holy Spirit. You told me, "Ken, when you make a mistake (and I did), remember, He still saw fit to save you. He knows your future better than your past and He still saves us in spite of us!"

Preface

Every day we are bombarded with advertisements and reality shows that in all *reality* don't teach us anything positive. We gain their understandings and perceptions on what their world looks like on a day to day basis, and although most of the shows are amazingly entertaining, they hold no eternal truth, or eternal value. Jesus says in John 8:32, *"You will know the truth and the truth will make you free."* The truth will cause freedom to come into your life. One of the mistruths in society is that Jesus was just a good man, a very moral man who taught us to treat others as we want to be treated. Others say that He was a great prophet or the greatest prophet that ever existed. Some say He was a heretic, a false rabbi who created the fastest growing gentile religion in the world. But like Peter, Jesus asked me the question "who do you say that I am"? At first I was just comfortable saying He is the Savior and Lord of all those who would receive him. But, after further consideration, He is more than a Savior, a good man, or a great prophet. Jesus is God from Genesis to Revelation and He appears as the Word throughout scripture. Not only does He appear as the Word, but that's also the name that He used in heaven before He took on the name Jesus. Literally the Angels called Him the Word of The Lord. I don't know when they saw Him if they said, "Hello Word," but I'm positive through scripture that Jesus is the Word, He is God, and it can be proven line upon line, precept upon precept, here a little and there a little. In reading the pages of this book my prayer is that you gain a deeper love and admiration for the Word because He is truly God and the entire book is about Him! Enjoy!!!!!!
Pastor Ken Johnson . . . Life Changers 4ever
www.lcchurch.us

6

Chapter 1
His Name is The Word!

John 8:56-58 Your father Abraham rejoiced to see my day: and he saw *it*, and was glad. Then said the Jews unto him, Thou art not yet fifty years old, and hast thou seen Abraham? Jesus said unto them, Verily, verily, I say unto you, Before Abraham was, I am. These words on a hot summer night challenged me to find out through scripture how that Jesus could make the claim he was the Great I Am! In doing so, I stumbled upon a revelation in the Word looking for answers about the Great I Am that led me to another name for the pre-incarnate Christ that will forever change history concerning Jesus name before he took on the name Jesus. In John 1 He declares "In the beginning was the Word and the Word was with God and the Word was God"! It is the Word that was made flesh. Jesus name in Heaven is the Word. The angels call him the Word of the Lord in their recounting of biblical history to Moses and other major and Minor Prophets and this Word has always existed Hallelujah. Jesus is the Word and that Word is God that Word is the great I Am! The all knowing The All Seeing God El Shaddai the Almighty God. In the text Jesus is talking with religious leaders about how truly far away they were from God and how that even though they had religion their father was the devil!

Jesus makes a statement in John 8:54 Jesus answered, if I honour myself, my honour is nothing: it is my Father that honoureth me; of whom ye say that he is your God: John 8:55 Yet ye have not known him; but I know him: and if I should say, I know him not, I shall be a liar like unto you: but I know him, and keep his saying. The religious people of Jesus time and even in this time have a form of Godliness but many have never experienced the hand of God, the power of God or have never experienced the face of God. I'm writing this book not to bash any group of people, not to down any ones denomination or religion. I'm writing this book to show to the Jew that Jesus is Messiah from the Torah. To show the Jehovah witness that He is Jehovah and to show the world that He is the everlasting Father. He has always existed and will always exist and that he has appeared to man from the beginning of time. It was Jesus in the garden walking with Adam in the cool of the day; it was Jesus who judged Cain after he slew his brother Abel and it was Jesus who preached the Gospel unto Abraham that caused him to believe unto righteousness. In my studies I have come across systematic theology that proves the bible is the inerrant word of God and that Jesus is not only the Son of God, he is The Lord, he is The Almighty, he is the Great I am and that He is the Word of the Lord, The Word of God and The Word just to name a few of his titles.

I will prove by several witnesses that Jesus name before He took on the name of Jesus in Heaven, His name was The Word, the angels called Him the word of the Lord. Man calls Him the Lord God. I will prove that many times we have not studied the bible correctly in talking about the Word of the Lord as just being prophesy or utterance we have missed key parts of the text that The Word of the Lord on many occasions is not prophesy at all but the appearing of Jesus Christ pre incarnate. That's not to say on many occasions the Word of the Lord wasn't prophesy because it was but The Word of the Lord is a person and that Word revealed Himself to Abraham and many of the old testament prophets throughout scripture and then to us in

John 1:1 when John declares by the spirit. **John 1:1** In the beginning was the Word, and the Word was with God, and the Word was God.

Notice the text says, In the beginning was the Word! And the Word was with God! And The Word Was God. The Word Was God, the Word is God and the Word will always be God. This text is dynamic for preaching, it is used by great orators around the globe for centuries, it has sparked the hearts of humanity and lit ablaze churches and crusades around the world but yet it's so much deeper than a great text to preach from. It's literally revelation of who Jesus was, is and will always be. It is revealing to mankind what his name is in heaven. 1 John **5:7** For there are three that bear record in heaven, the Father, the Word, and the Holy Ghost: and these three are one.
In no way am I taking away from the Trinity in their oneness. I believe That God is one and that he manifest throughout the bible in the face of Jesus Christ who is The Word. I believe when we get to heaven there will be one throne and after Jesus has come and said the words we all long to hear, Well done thou Good and Faithful Servant is that He will go and sit on His throne enveloped by His Fathers glory and the Father The Word and The Spirit will be one. The Only difference is the body that He prepared will throughout all eternity show the sacrifice He made when the Word became flesh and dwelt amongst us. We will forever see in his hands the nail prints, the hole in His side, the stripes on his back and the flesh that has been glorified so that we could experience glory.

Chapter Two
The Encounter and the Call

Now the LORD had said unto Abram, Get thee out of thy country, and from thy kindred, and from thy father's house, unto a land that I will shew thee: and I will make of thee a great nation, and I will bless thee, and make thy name great; and thou shalt be a blessing: and I will bless them that bless thee, and curse him that curseth thee: and in thee shall all families of the earth be blessed. So Abram departed, as the LORD had spoken unto him; and Lot went with him: and Abram was seventy and five years old when he departed out of Haran. (Genesis 12:1-4)

What makes a man leave his comfort zone, move away from what he's used to, leave the people he loves the most, and walk away from his family? Leave the worshipping of the moon god, walk away from paganism and idolatry? I can tell you easily. It's an encounter with God—not just any god, but the true and the living God. A touch of the Master's hand, a face to face meeting with divinity, an offer that cannot be refused, twisted, or compromised. A promise of blessings by the Blessor. The God who created heaven and earth comes and manifests himself to a man who at this time was not a Jew. As a matter of fact, there was no Jewish race physically as it was they were still in his loins. He was not the father of any, yet alone many would be the promise. Abraham was in Haran with his family and with his wife enjoying life when the Lord appears to him and says to him, "Get out of your comfort zone, leave your city, your region, your neighborhood.

Not only that, but leave your kinfolk, walk away from the relationships you've built and established all of these years. Do not just leave your cousins, aunts, uncles and your friends, but leave your father's house. Right about there I'm confident fear gripped him for a moment. He knew nothing about faith he had no scripture on which he could rely. There wasn't any scripture. He couldn't name it or claim it, confess it or possess it, yet he knew that this person who appeared to him had the power to change his life forever. I've come to find out through experience that if you're going to follow God with your whole heart you have to be willing to obey Him when it's painful, or inconvenient. Even when you don't know your next move, you know you got a word from God and it's time to move. He has nations on his mind. He has greatness He wants to birth, blessings He wants to release, and people He wants to reach. You have to be willing to follow Him and be willing to give up all of your current comforts, luxuries, and people in order to fulfill the will of God.

I'm sure for Abraham as it would be for anyone, it was difficult to leave a place where you are successful and living in the best conditions. You have a nice home, you drive a nice car, you're experiencing success— you already have prosperity without God. As a matter of fact, you're doing well without a word, without church, without tithing. Life is good and now a God who I've never met before, whose ways I am oblivious to, and whose commands confuse me appears and says, "Leave all of this and the people you love the most and go to a land that I'm going to show you later!" Most people would say, "This has to be a nightmare! This can't be real. It has to be a dream." Yet Abraham, at the promise of God through His appearing, decided to alter the course of his life and history as we

11

know it. He took the leap of faith and left Haran and his father's house to start out on a journey with the true and living God.

So Abram departed, as the LORD had spoken unto him; and Lot went with him: and Abram was seventy and five years old when he departed out of Haran. (Genesis 12:4) At the time when most people are retired and ready to live off the fruit of their labor, for the remainder of there years Abram departed as the Lord spoke unto him, and even though Jesus said Abraham rejoiced to see His day and he saw it and was glad, we see Abraham moving in partial obedience instead of full obedience. The Bible says in Genesis 12:4, *"So Abram departed, as the LORD had spoken unto him; and Lot went with him."* This is another book in itself—to deal with being in God's perfect will, but we see Abram answering the call partially, for the Bible says that Lot went with him. That statement should never exist. It is the cause of unending pain for Lot, his family, and for Abraham. Remember the call to Abraham at the appearing of the Lord?

Now the LORD had said unto Abram, Get thee out of thy country, and from thy kindred, (Lot) and from thy father's house, unto a land that I will shew thee: God has a desire to show us things He has planned for us. He wants to show us a place He has prepared for the believer, and to show us the life He has in mind for us. God wants to reveal it all, but many times it takes the first steps of obedience, and when we obey Him fully we experience our promised land. I believe this book is a step of faith for me that will unlock every promises he has made to the believer. But, first we must obey and get the Lot's out of our lives. This book has been on the shelf.

For more than a decade, while I've journeyed through my own path and partially obeyed the Lord, this revelation that can and will free the conservative Jew, show the Witness that Jesus is Jehovah, and show the world they can count on the Savior who was and is and will always be the Word of the Lord, has been locked up. Abram met Him in Genesis 12 and you will experience the Word like you never have before. Take a moment and pray with me before going further.

Prayer:
God, give me the spirit of wisdom and revelation, open the eyes of my understanding, and teach me in-depth about the everlasting power of Jesus. Father, teach me how to understand the Word! The One who has always existed, the One who is concerned with the fulfillment of my destiny and purpose being fulfilled. Father, teach me His ways so I can enjoy His presence, His presents, and His success being released over my life. Father, open the eyes of my heart. Flood me with your light. I believe and I receive it in Jesus name.

Chapter Three
The Word Preaches to Abraham

Your father Abraham rejoiced to see my day: and he saw it, and was glad. Then said the Jews unto him, Thou art not yet fifty years old, and hast thou seen Abraham? Jesus said unto them, Verily, verily, I say unto you, Before Abraham was, I am. (John 8:56-58)
Even as Abraham believed God, and it was accounted to him for righteousness. Know ye therefore that they which are of faith, the same are the children of Abraham. And the scripture, foreseeing that God would justify the heathen through faith, preached before the gospel unto Abraham, saying, In thee shall all nations be blessed. (Gal 3:6-8)

Jesus testifies to the Pharisees that Abraham rejoiced to see His day and was glad. That's an amazing statement to make from a man who was barely past the age of 30, and He's talking about a relationship that He had with a man that would have lived over 2000 years prior. Religious people are looking at Jesus thinking, "Yeah right." In their minds He is a lunatic. He is crazy, and many of us would have thought the same thing. It is humanly impossible to say that we have ever met someone who is 2000 years old because the span of a man's life is much less than 100 years old. Jesus, after so kindly disrupting there fleshly thinking, goes on to say, *"Verily verily I say unto you, before Abraham was I am."* I am God, Jesus was saying. Let's not beat around the bush or go around the corner with this matter. I Am that I Am. I don't need your approval. I don't need you to validate me. I'm not asking for your stamp or permission to preach.

I am God and I met Abraham and I preached the Good news to Abraham and every person that believes in me is blessed in faithful Abraham. He becomes righteous because he believed in the Lord. That's good news, not just for them, but for us also. By believing in the Lord, we can still be made righteous before God. *"And if you be Christ's then are you Abrahams Seed and heirs according to the promise." (Galatians 3:29)* The Lord shows up in Abraham's life in Genesis chapter 12 and He gives him specific instructions on what he is to do in order to become blessed and the father of many nations.

Now the LORD had said unto Abram, Get thee out of thy country, and from thy kindred, and from thy father's house, unto a land that I will shew thee: And I will make of thee a great nation, and I will bless thee, and make thy name great; and thou shalt be a blessing" (Gen 12:1-2

This is part and parcel of the Gospel. It is good news and we partake of this blessing and we understand God blesses us with believing Abraham so that we can be blessed to be a blessing. However, let's take it a step further. I want to show you Jesus in a different facet in Genesis 12. God appears to Abraham as the Lord. Now the book of Genesis is written not by Abraham but by Moses. He actually has the book given to him by the hand of Angels. Genesis cannot be Moses' perspective because he was not there; he had yet to be born.

Wherefore then serveth the law? It was added because of transgressions, till the seed should come to whom the promise was made; and it was Ordained by Angels in the hand of a Mediator. (Gal 3:19)

Who have received the Law by the disposition of Angels, and have not kept it. (Acts 7:53)

Genesis is God's perspective transcribed first hand by Angels who were assigned to Abraham. They came back and gave the accounts of the stories that took place in Genesis. Moses hadn't even come on the scene. So, we are getting God's angelic insight into what happened, who were the participants, and what they called God. Humans would say, "This is the Lord God," or "the Lord. That was their salutation. The angels on the other hand called Him something totally different. They called Him the Lord God, "the Word of the Lord," and we took it to mean that the prophetic gift was in place or in motion when all along it was not prophecy in most instances, but it was the Word appearing to His prophetic candidates to give them covenant instructions or scrolls to chew on. How can you be a prophet if the term has yet to be given?

How can you prophesy and you don't even know what it means to be a prophet? You would need an introductory course by a qualified teacher who had mastered the gift himself. It's like calling a person a chef who has never cooked in his life. He needs someone to teach him culinary arts in order to qualify him. So, how can Abram get the Word of the Lord, say what God says, go back and put in a book without a pen, computer, or the internet, and remember verbatim every word that came to him? Now, I have an excellent memory. I can remember a lot of things, but I cannot remember a conversation I had even yesterday where I can recite everything that I said or that someone else said to me with divine accuracy. *I* can't. Perhaps you can. But, for the average person who gets a word from God (if it's not recorded on tape (DVD or CD) it's nearly impossible for you to go back and write down word for word what was said if it was more than a few words, especially without a pen, voice recorder, or a

16

camcorder. We have missed out on the true prophets' ministry of a seer by making everything utterance based, but I beg to differ. Most prophets in the Old Testament were not prophets because they could prophesy, but were prophets because they saw God. They were seers, that's why the scripture found in proverbs that says where there is no vision the people perish has really been used out of context. I've been guilty of preaching that it's about vision and how you need a vision for your life. You do need a vision for your life, but that's not what the text actually says. It says, "Where there is no prophetic vision the people perish," meaning where the prophet has not seen and heard from God, the people will perish. A true prophet had an encounter with God where He appeared as the Word of the Lord and He gave them instructions, insight, scrolls and power.

After these things the word of the LORD came unto Abram in a vision, saying, Fear not, Abram: I am thy shield, and thy exceeding great reward. (Genesis 15:1) What brings the Word on the scene? How do I get God to show up in my situations? I'm glad you asked because the key is found in the prior verses it's called the power of confession.

Look at what moved God to appear unto Abraham then we look at the Word like we have never seen him before.

And the king of Sodom said unto Abram, Give me the persons, and take the goods to thyself. And Abram said to the king of Sodom, I have lift up mine hand unto the LORD, the most high God, the possessor of heaven and earth, that I will not take from a thread even to a shoe latchet, and that I will not take any thing that is thine, lest thou shouldest say, I have made Abram rich: (Genesis 14:21-23)

17

In Genesis 14 we see Abraham defeating four Kingdoms with 318 trained men from his own house in order to go and rescue lot and his family back from captivity. Not only does he get Lot back, but, he gets back all of the king of Sodom's goods and persons. The king then tries to bless Abraham and says that he can have all of the stuff, all of the goods. Just give back the people, the families that were taken. Abram makes an extraordinary statement, especially for the people of God. It doesn't matter if you are the preacher or the prophet. It's hard to turn down a blessing that big when offered. But, look at Abram's response that moves God to appear unto him and to offer him a covenant that would bless all nations and future generations who would receive Christ.

And Abram said to the king of Sodom, I have lift up mine hand unto the LORD, the most high God, the possessor of heaven and earth, that I will not take from a thread even to a shoe latchet, and that I will not take any thing that is thine, lest thou shouldest say, I have made Abram rich: (Gen 14:22-23)

Abram says I have given God my oath that I will not take from a thread to a shoe latchet from you. I will not take any thing that is yours lest you get the credit for the blessing in my life. You or your sinful people will not get credit for saying you made me rich. That's not to say that God doesn't use the wealth of the sinner to bring wealth transference. That's not to say He doesn't touch the heart of people and get them to give into your bosom. But, on this occasion Abram made it clear to the wicked king of Sodom, "I don't want anything that you possess and I didn't go to get your stuff. I went and fought to get my family back."

This declaration of faith in God acknowledges Him as being his provider, and confesses his absolute trust and faith in God and not in man. God shows up to bless Abram and there's a principle revealed in this. Sometimes God wants you to trust in Him, not in other people, their abilities, or their bank accounts. He wants you to trust Him and declare it in the face of wealth and adversity that no one will say that they made you rich, but your trust is in the Lord. That type of faith and confidence moves the person of God to show up in your situation.

After these things the word of the LORD came unto Abram in a vision, saying, Fear not, Abram: I am thy shield, and thy exceeding great reward. **(Gen 15:1)** Understand that the Bible was not written in verse and chapter by God. We have a transitioned from chapter 14 which closes the confession of Abraham's faith in God. This now brings God on the scene and we can see how Abraham would rejoice and how the Gospel will be preached unto him. Abraham has the Word to show up in his life.

When I saw this scripture it jumped out at me and God began to speak to me. He began to ask me questions like "How does a Word show up in a vision?" In the natural mind we may see words floating in mid air with a message to others. We may see a Wall Street ticker tape scrolling across the screen. We may see green screen and video editing techniques to make the words appear, but there is no software, TV, internet, or led screens. There are no Hollywood special effects. The Bible says the Word of the Lord Came unto Abram in a vision. Most Bible scholars would make this out to be prophecy, but this is not prophecy, nor is it the first act of prophecy in the Bible. This is the Word appearing before it was made flesh.

This is the Word that is God and the Word that will always be God. This is the angels' name for Jesus before He is called Jesus. Remember, the book is being mediated by the hands of angels from the angels' point of view. Moses was not there to experience what Abram is seeing. So, the angels write and relay to Moses this message found in the Torah.

After these things the word of the LORD came unto Abram in a vision, saying, Fear not, Abram: I am thy shield, and thy exceeding great reward. **(Gen 15:1)**

And if it was prophesied in a prophetic utterance, why would the Word tell us not to fear anything. That which is relayed would not make you afraid it would make you rejoice. I am thy shield (thy protector the one who fights your battles) I am your exceeding great reward. I am your rapidly coming increase. If it's prophecy alone there's no reason to fear. It's time to rejoice, hallelujah, that's a good word of protection and increase.

But, it's not prophecy; it's the appearing of Jesus preaching the good news unto Abraham *"Abraham rejoiced to see my day and he saw it."(John 8:58)*

Now we have to take our time and look at the text closely and see why He would have to tell him not to be afraid.

After these things the word of the LORD came unto Abram in a vision, saying, Fear not, Abram: I am thy shield, and thy exceeding great reward. **(Genesis 15:1)**

Abraham is afraid of his presence the Word appears to him. I don't know if He was wrapped in Glory or in flames. I don't know what His person looked like, but I'm sure if God or an angel appeared unto you at first there would be fear, shock, awe, and amazement. Then there would have been reverence worship and adorations.

20

Abram understood that the Word wanted to make covenant with him. He understood that when the Lord said, "I am thy shield and thy exceeding great reward," that He's coming to make a covenant with him. That's why in the midst of this open vision he said, "Lord God." That's what he (Abram) calls Him, Lord God, Jehovah God. But remember, this is being transcribed from the eyes of an angel. So, Abram says, "Lord God, what will you give me?" He knows that if covenant is being offered that there is an exchange that's going to make his life better. He was already rich, but when you're in covenant with a stronger party, all of their provision, protection, and power become yours. You gain access. So, Abram says in Genesis 15:2, "You got all of this stuff you want to give me, but I go childless. Look God, the only person I can leave all of these possessions to is this Eliezer of Damascus. He is the closest thing I have to a child. He will inherit everything at my death. *"And Abram said, Lord GOD, what wilt thou give me, seeing I go childless, and the steward of my house is this Eliezer of Damascus?*

Abram talking with the Word of the Lord Says, "Look at me. I have no seed. I have no way to reproduce. My loins are barren. I'm shooting blanks. I have no children.

And Abram said, Behold; to me thou hast given no seed: and, lo, one born in my house is mine heir. And, behold, the word of the LORD came unto him, saying, this shall not be thine heir; but he that shall come forth out of thine own bowels shall be thine heir. (Gen 15:3-4)
Now he's talking to a man in his senior years that hasn't produced any children yet he's past the age of physical reproduction and the Word says no this blessing is coming from your body.

Can I stop right here and tell you it doesn't matter what it looks like in your body or in your life right now? The blessing is going to come out of your life and it's going to affect your children's children. This blessing is for you and no devil, ailment, or past failures are going to stop what God has ordained for you.

Have you ever had the Word walk you outside? This made me shout because when you look at Genesis 15:1, it says the Word of the Lord appears unto Abram in a vision and now the Word becomes a He!

And He (The Word of the Lord) brought him forth abroad, and said, look now toward heaven, and tell the stars, if thou be able to number them: and He said unto him, So shall thy seed be. (Gen 15:5)

The Word of The Lord, Jesus, preached the Gospel to Abraham and spent quality time with him as heaven invaded the Earth. He walked Him outside and says, "Look, with your eyes towards the consolation and count the stars if you can." The Word tells him that's how big his blessing is going to be. That's how many natural and supernatural kids you're going to birth. He is a man in the flesh who doesn't have any children, but in the Spirit Realm, in the mind of God he has more than he can count. I'm here to tell you that all you need is a Word from God to change your situation. It has been said that one Word from God can change your life forever, and one gift from God can set you forever. The Word is still speaking and He's saying that if you be Christ's then are You Abraham's seed and heirs according to the promise. (See Galatians 3:26)

Your father Abraham rejoiced to see my day: and he saw it, and was glad. (John 8:56)

And the Gospel was preached unto Abram and the bible says. *And he believed in the LORD; and he counted it to him for righteousness. (Gen 15:6)*

The Gospel demands belief and when we believe and we receive His Word he will make us Righteous he will give us Right Standing So I can stand in his presences as though I've never sinned.

And I will make of thee a great nation, and I will bless thee, and make thy name great; and thou shalt be a blessing: and I will bless them that bless thee, and curse him that curseth thee: and in thee shall all families of the earth be blessed. (Genesis 12:2-3)

Chapter Four
The Word Appears to Samuel

The Word appears to Samuel in 1Sam 3:1 *"And the child Samuel ministered unto the LORD before Eli. And the word of the LORD was precious in those days; there was no open vision."* The child Samuel at this time was not operating in the office of a prophet at the time. He was serving under the man of God, the great priest Eli, who had fallen himself out of favor with God because he would not judge the blatant sins of his sons, Hophni and Phineas. The Word was not appearing. He was not manifesting to his men of God. The scriptures tell us that the Word of the Lord was precious in those days. Literally, it says, "no open vision." God would not appear to his priest, but He would not discount the needs of the nation. Where one will not do what the Word says do, He will raise up someone else who will. It's very important that we stay glued to the text, for in the text a mystery will be revealed. But, we must be studious and meditative in order to grasp this eternal truth.

And it came to pass at that time, when Eli was laid down in his place, and his eyes began to wax dim, that he could not see . . ." (1Sam 3:2)
Eli the Priest had become blind physically and spiritually because he would not Judge sin in his house, the sin that was effecting the house and the people of God. It's funny how when one is sin sick it will produce physical symptoms in one's life. Eli is the spiritual head of the house of God and he is the spiritual and physical leader of his sons who serve in ministry with him. His refusal to Judge them caused judgment to come upon him and it caused a season of no fresh bread in the house of God.

No manna, revelation, anointing, no presence, and no power. His disobedience affected him physically and spiritually, but it also affected the entire nation of Israel. Look at 1Sam 3:1 b. *"And the word of the LORD was precious in those days; there was no open vision."* It's never good when God does not talk with his people or to his priest. They were in a famine and didn't know it. The sad reality is many churches and pastors and wonderful people of God have gotten comfortable being in a place where God *did* speak instead of being in a place where God *is* speaking. And people are more faithful to a past movement than they are to a current move of God. If that's you, pray and ask God to send you to a place where there is fresh bread hot out of Heaven's ovens. The Word says in John 7:37, *"In the last day, that great day of the feast, Jesus stood and cried, saying, if any man thirst, let him come unto me, and drink. The Word was there all alone."*

  "And ere the lamp of God went out in the temple of the LORD, where the ark of God was, and Samuel was laid down to sleep . . ." (1Sam 3:3)

  Samuel is resting from his duties in the temple for the evening when God is ready to bring about promotion in his life and ministry. At this point Samuel does not know God for himself. He has not appeared unto him in a personal way. He is the servant of *Eli* in the house of God, and God wants to make him the servant of *God* in the house of God. How much more effective could the church be if we could get the members, the leaders, and the priests to serve God in the house of God? Not only serve the preacher, but to have a heart to Serve God under the direction of the man of God. Too often we miss out on God's best, serving in the house of God, but not serving God. God calls Samuel and he thinks its Eli voice he hears.

25

And ere the lamp of God went out in the temple of the LORD, where the ark of God was, and Samuel was laid down to sleep; that the LORD called Samuel: and he answered, here am I. And he ran unto Eli, and said, Here am I; for thou calledst me. (1Sam. 3:3-5)

Samuel thinks the priest Eli is calling him and so he runs to his teacher to see what he wants and he said, *"I called not; lie down again. And he went and lay down."* By this time in the story Samuel may think he is losing his mind. He is hearing voices and he's going to Eli to answer the call, but Eli is not the one calling. Can I tell some of you that man is not the one calling you, but God is— He will use men to teach you and to train you. God calls you to ministry, not men. We can recognize gifts in you and anointings on your life, but at the end of the day you want a ministry that was God called and God ordained. It is then that no flesh can glory in his presence.

Let's look at 1Samuel 3:6 *"And the LORD called yet again . . ."* God is persistent. He is trying to get Samuel's attention, so, God ramps up the call and He calls him again, *"Samuel. And Samuel arose and went to Eli, and said, "Here am I; for thou didst call me. And he answered, I called not, my son; lie down again."* By this time Samuel is thinking, "Ok, what's really going on? I'm hearing someone calling me, yet, when I go to who I think it is who called he says that it's not his voice I'm hearing. We find out a secret in Samuel's life right here. Even though he was serving in the house of God and faithful in his church attendance, he did not yet know the Lord. The Word of the Lord (Jesus) hadn't appeared unto him. *"Now Samuel did not yet know the LORD, an either was the word of the LORD yet revealed unto him."* (1Samuel 3:7)

The Word of the Lord hadn't made His appearance to Samuel before this he appeared previously in Eli's ministry. Sin brought a disconnect in his life and ministry now He is looking for someone else who will say yes to His will and yes to His ministry "*And the LORD called Samuel again the third time.*" (1Samuel 3:8) Wow, three times the Word is calling Him and he runs to Eli. There has to come a place in every believer's life where they make a decision to hear from God for themselves. It's not just going to the preacher or getting in a prayer line and being lathered up with oil. It's taking the time out to make a quality decision—I am going to get to know God for myself. "*And he arose and went to Eli, and said, Here am I; for thou didst call me. And Eli perceived that the LORD had called the child.*" Eli then perceives that the same way that the Word came into his life is the same experience now that's happening to Samuel. So, he gives him some godly wisdom: *Therefore Eli said unto Samuel, Go, and lie down: and it shall be, if He calls thee, (the word of the Lord) that thou shalt say, Speak, LORD; for thy servant heareth. (1Samuel 3:9)*

Samuel went and lay down in his place. Eli gives him simple instructions. He tells him that when he hears the voice again to say, "Speak Lord For thy servant heareth." Look at 1Sameuel 3:10. "*And the LORD came, and Stood, and called as at other times.*" God came to him God stood right next to him. He was right in the room with him all along and Samuel was off somewhere else trying to find God. Notice it says "And the Lord came and the Lord Stood . . ." He wants to manifest himself in our lives. He wants to stand with and live big in us and through us, but He needs a "Yes Lord!" God is shouting, "Samuel, Samuel!" Then, Samuel answered, *"Speak; for thy servant heareth."*

And the LORD said to Samuel, Behold, I will do a thing in Israel, at which both the ears of every one that heareth it shall tingle. "In that day I will perform against Eli all things which I have spoken concerning his house: when I begin, I will also make an end. For I have told him that I will judge his house for ever for the iniquity which he knoweth; because his sons made themselves vile, and he restrained them not. And therefore I have sworn unto the house of Eli, that the iniquity of Eli's house shall not be purged with sacrifice nor offering forever. And Samuel lay until the morning, and opened the doors of the house of the LORD. And Samuel feared to shew Eli the Vision." *(1Samuel 3:12-15)*

Notice, Samuel feared to Shew Eli the Vision. This wasn't prophecy, this wasn't utterance, this was a vision where God suspended the natural course of his life and intervened. He appeared unto Samuel at his, *"Speak Lord, thy Servant Heareth"* at that salutation and manifested Himself. This is his first encounter with the Word of the Lord. It's interesting to note that this must have been a practice of introduction with God concerning his priest and Prophets. God would appear unto them and give them instructions and insight. God literally put the beginning priest and prophets in his own training school where He was the teacher. How else would they prophesy if He hadn't instructed them? How else could they proclaim if he hadn't appeared to them? So, a prophet in the days of old had an encounter where they would see God, and He would minister to them on a personal level and give them instruction and place the word of God in their mouths. This is why many prophets were called seers, because they saw into the Spirit realm. Many of the prophets literally saw God. Take a look at 1Samuel 3:16. *"Then Eli called*

Samuel, and said, Samuel, my son. And he answered, Here am I." Notice how Samuel knows the difference this time. After having a true encounter with God you will know the difference between His voice and other voices that may be in your life.

"And he said, What is the thing that the LORD hath said unto thee? I pray thee hide it not from me: God do so to thee and more also, if thou hide anything from me of all the things that he said unto thee." *(1Samuel 3:17)*

Eli Knows God has appeared instructed and left orders. *"And Samuel told him every whit, and hid nothing from him. And he said, It is the LORD: let him do what seemeth him good. And Samuel grew, and the LORD was with him, and did let none of his words fall to the ground. And all Israel from Dan even to Beersheba knew that Samuel was established to be a prophet of the LORD. And the LORD appeared again in Shiloh: for the LORD revealed himself to Samuel in Shiloh by the Word of the LORD."* (1Samuel 3:18-19)

Samuel gives up the privied information to his mentor that in any realm is grievous and Eli Knows once God has spoken there is no reversing his actions. If God said it then that settles it and there is no reversing his order. Samuel is established as a Prophet before the people and the way that the people knew Samuel was a true prophet is because God didn't allow any of his words to fall to the Ground. *"And the Lord appeared again in Shiloh: The LORD reveals himself to Samuel in Shiloh by The Word of the Lord."* Samuel knew the Word. He had sat at his feet and was mentored in his presence The Word appeared to him throughout his ministry. Jesus as we know him today appeared in whatever form as the Word of the Lord.

Chapter Five
The Word that came to Jeremiah

"The words of Jeremiah the son of Hilkiah, of the priests that were in Anathoth in the land of Benjamin: To whom the word of the LORD came in the days of Josiah the son of Amon king of Judah, in the thirteenth year of his reign. It came also in the days of Jehoiakim the son of Josiah king of Judah, unto the end of the eleventh year of Zedekiah the son of Josiah king of Judah, unto the carrying away of Jerusalem captive in the fifth month. Then the word of the LORD came unto me, saying, Before I formed thee in the belly I knew thee; and before thou camest forth out of the womb I sanctified thee, and I ordained thee a prophet unto the nations. Then said I, Ah, Lord GOD! Behold, I cannot speak: for I am a child. But the LORD said unto me, Say not, I am a child: for thou shalt go to all that I shall send thee, and whatsoever I command thee thou shalt speak. Be not afraid of their faces: for I am with thee to deliver thee, saith the LORD. Then the LORD put forth his hand, and touched my mouth. And the LORD said unto me, Behold, I have put my words in thy mouth. See, I have this day set thee over the nations and over the kingdoms, to root out, and to pull down, and to destroy, and to throw down, to build, and to plant." (Jeremiah 1:1-10)

The Word of the Lord comes to Jeremiah in this text and it seems that whenever the Word appears to new prophets, in order to place them in the office in which they have been recruited and called tot it seems, the Word appears to them and gives them specific instructions to the call and assignment that is given unto them. Let's look a little deeper into the text beginning at Jeremiah 1: 4.

Then the word of the LORD came unto me, saying, Before I formed thee in the belly I knew thee; and before thou camest forth out of the womb I sanctified thee, and I ordained thee a prophet unto the nations. (Jeremiah 1:4-5) Notice that the Word of the Lord came "saying".

30

Great insight into the relationship we possess with God and how before we entered get into our mother's womb He knew us. He had a relationship with us. He has had conversations with us and before we ever come into the world. Our purpose is built into us and the calling of God is placed upon us. With DNA specific to the assignment is given to us and that God will do whatever it takes to get us in position in order to fulfill the destiny that's on the inside of us. I now have a better understanding of Proverbs 19:21. *"Many are the plans in a man's heart, but it is the LORD's purpose that prevails."* Great insight, but there's more. He now drops the prophet title and status on a child (perhaps teenager) who before this encounter was living his life as he saw fit. Now he meets God in the face of the Word of the Lord. Now he is given instruction by God in a face to face conversation.

Most theologians and preachers would say that he got a prophetic utterance from the Lord. The Spirit of God was upon him and he began to prophesy and receive transmission from Gods spirit into the prophets heart which registers in his mind and he then speaks what thus saith the Lord. But I want to refute that openly, using the scripture because this young man was not a prophet. He was not familiar with the move of God. He was not familiar with the Anointing— Gods Super upon a man's Natural. As you keep reading, he says "I am just a little kid. I don't know what to do or how to talk to your people."

"Then said I, Ah, Lord GOD! Behold, I cannot speak: for I am a child. But the LORD said unto me, Say no, I am a child: for thou shalt go to all that I shall send thee, and whatsoever I command thee thou shalt speak." (Jeremiah 1:6-7) As with any person thrown into a new profession without formal training, there will be some fear and some anxiety. Try showing up the first day at United airlines and they tell you to go to the cockpit. You're going to fly this plane not simulate, but fly. There will be some reservations, fear, and trepidation because you're not use to flying

you've never done it before. Jeremiah talked to God face to face and said, "I am not prepared for this assignment, nor in my mind can I handle what you're asking me to do." Look at verses 7-8 of the text.

But the LORD said unto me, Say not, I am a child: for thou shalt go to all that I shall send thee, and whatsoever I command thee thou shalt speak. Be not afraid of their faces: for I am with thee to deliver thee, saith the LORD. What a promise to a novice prophet. Don't worry about what to say or how to operate in the gift of the prophetic. "Whatever I command you to say that will you speak. and another thing, Jeremiah, people are going to look at you as if you are crazy, and talk even crazier to you because they won't think you are qualified because of your age and your experience. But you have this guarantee from me. *"Be not afraid of their faces: for I am with thee to deliver thee, saith the LORD."* Now for most prophets, preachers, or people for that matter, that's a deal you can't refuse. God is going to be with me to deliver me no matter how bad the odds are stacked against me. As a pastor I'm in, but the story line gets better. Pay attention to verse 9. *"Then the LORD put forth his hand, and touched my mouth. And the LORD said unto me, Behold, I have put my words in thy mouth."*

This verse further solidified in my heart that the Word of the Lord was the pre-incarnate Jesus—the Word that became flesh and took a body for all mankind's redemption. Look closely, *"Then the Lord put forth his hand."* Now the Word is present externally in this beginning book of Jeremiah. He puts forth a hand. I have prophesied and preached for several years now and I've never seen a physical hand come out of my spirit or out of the Bible that touched my mouth. Now, I have been quickened and I have been anointed and divinely energized. I have had the Spirit of God move in me, all over me, be upon me, and the move of God has blessed my church and other congregations. However, I've never had the Word put forth His hand and touch my Mouth.

It's evident that the Word of the Lord is in the room the Lord God. He touches his mouth. He puts His Word on the inside of his newly manifested prophet. God appears to him personally with power and revelation and Words that he puts inside of the prophet. This is pre-salvation, pre-resurrection, pre-Pentecost. The Holy Spirit didn't live inside of Jeremiah like it does the New Testament believer, yet, Jeremiah has an encounter with God that guarantees that he will have the victory and that God will be with him to deliver him.

Wow, what a promise! What an encounter! What a touch to have the hand of God literally touch the prophets mouth and place his words on the inside! It's more clear how the prophets of old could prophesy, then go and find parchment paper, get ink, create a pen, then write precisely what thus saith the Lord without a recorder, DVD, or internet. The Word Himself put the Word inside of the prophet's mouths, and then gives him comfort and training and then promises to be there when he needs them most. "And the Lord Said unto me behold I have put my Words in thy mouth."

Chapter Six
The Word that Came to Ezekiel

The Word that came to Ezekiel, as we study it next, we will
see further insight into how God moved upon some of the
prophets as He placed the scroll in Ezekiel's mouth. I
believe it was a common practice for the Word to have
them eat the scroll, therefore giving them the ability to
bring it back up when needed. *"So I opened my mouth, and
he fed me the scroll."* (Ezekiel 3:2)

As we have look further into the revelation of The
Word of the Lord, we notice a common thing that happened
to major and Minor Prophets when God would appear unto
them. He would appear as the Word of the Lord, in what
form I am not sure. At this time He doesn't have a body or
a man's name (Jesus) that He has taken on and exalted. As
God, He has the right to change forms and appearances as
He sees fit. I'm positive in different instances it must have
not been the exact representation of a man's form, because
Abraham was afraid of His presence, and Job was terrified
as well at the presence of God. It's my opinion that at times
He came looking similar to a man, but maybe more angelic,
but I'm sure that he was wrapped in some type of splendor
or a facet of His glory.

Moses knew God face to face and he lived. Joshua
saw him in the temple. In other manifestations I believe
that when God appeared to his prophets he showed them all
a view of what glory they could handle in their physical
bodies. He's the same God that told Moses no man shall
see my Glory and live. So, He shows Moses a glimpse of
his backside after hiding him in the cleft of the Rock. In the
same breadth He showed his prophets enough of His God
factor to cause them to leave family, friends, and loved
ones to go into nations and claim them at His direction as
well as prophesy to nations, other prophets, and people at
the direction of the Word of the Lord. It made a child
prophet like Jeremiah move out at the direction of the Word

and prophesy and weep to his people, all at the instructions of the Word of the Lord.

The Word that came to Ezekiel

"The word of the LORD came expressly unto Ezekiel the priest, the son of Buzi, in the land of the Chaldeans by the river Chebar; and the hand of the LORD was there upon him. And I looked, and, behold, a whirlwind came out of the north, a great cloud, and a fire enfolding itself, and brightness was about it, and out of the midst thereof as the color of amber, out of the midst of the fire. Also out of the midst thereof came the likeness of four living creatures. And this was their appearance; they had the likeness of a man. And every one had four faces, and every one had four wings. And their feet were straight feet; and the sole of their feet was like the sole of a calf's foot: and they sparkled like the color of burnished brass. And they had the hands of a man under their wings on their four sides; and they four had their faces and their wings.

Their wings were joined one to another; they turned not when they went; they went every one straight forward. As for the likeness of their faces, they four had the face of a man, and the face of a lion, on the right side: and they four had the face of an ox on the left side; they four also had the face of an eagle." (Ezekiel 1:3-10)

Ezekiel's Encounter with The Word of the Lord was based upon a supernatural vision that opened up the realms of the spirit and allowed Ezekiel to see not only the Word of the Lord (as we will see and tie it all in with later verses) but Ezekiel saw the living creatures in all of their splendor and glory, and multifaceted views having the shape of men and animals wrapped in flames of glory. The prophet experienced the Glory of the Lord and its protectors in all of its different facets. The bible says in verse 1, *"The word of the LORD came expressly unto Ezekiel the priest, the son of Buzi, in the land of the Chaldeans by the river Chebar; and the hand of the LORD was there upon him."*

35

God's hand was upon Ezekiel in a different way. It wasn't an introductory meeting with the Prophet but it was a journey in the spirit realm where God took him into the Spirit realm and showed him his glory and the glory of his creation. The way that he talked with Ezekiel was markedly different. Read verses 1-2 again.

And he said unto me, Son of man, stand upon thy feet, and I will speak unto thee. Eze. 2:2 And the spirit entered into me when he spake unto me, and set me upon my feet, that I heard him that spake unto me."

He tells Ezekiel to stand up. When he stands up the Spirit of God enters into Ezekiel and the power of God floors him to the degree that God has to prop him up in order to hold a conversation with him about the rebellious ways of His people of whom He wants to send Ezekiel to prophesy. In the text God speaks to him in detail about the rebelliousness of the people, and the rejection he will face. But, Ezekiel speaks what the Lord says anyway. God gives him the words to say, and then He places before His prophet a scroll that He puts in his mouth and makes him eat. We will pick up the story again in second chapter of Ezekiel. *"And when I looked, behold, a hand was sent unto me; and, lo, a roll of a book was therein; and he spread it before me; and it was written within and without: and there was written therein lamentations, and mourning, and woe."* (Ezekiel 2:9-10)

Notice, that the hand is present in verse 9 has a scroll in it. Now we would agree that most of the time when a hand is present in the Bible a body is generally present (outside of the time when a hand appears before the wicked king at what they deemed to be an outstanding party before the hand writing on the wall pronounces judgment, Daniel 5:5 NLT, *"Suddenly, they saw the fingers of a human hand writing on the plaster wall of the king's palace, near the lamp stand"*). The king himself saw the hand as it wrote. With that being said, Ezekiel is having a meeting with God and getting instructions directly from

36

Him, after getting his first round of verbal instructions on what he is to say to the rebellious people of Israel. He now has to get prepared to swallow the Word of God by the Word of Gods leading.

"Moreover he said unto me, Son of man, eat that thou findest; eat this roll, and go speak unto the house of Israel. So I opened my mouth, and he caused me to eat that roll. And he said unto me, Son of man, cause thy belly to eat, and fill thy bowels with this roll that I give thee. Then did I eat it; and it was in my mouth as honey for sweetness." (Ezekiel 3:1-3) *"So I opened my mouth and he caused me to eat that roll."*

This is not a dinner roll it's a scroll, and the prophet says and (He) the Word of the Lord, the Lord God, caused him to eat that roll. I don't know what the paper was made of. I don't know if it was covered in chocolate, but what I do know is that God put the Scroll in Ezekiel's mouth and He caused him to eat that roll. Ezekiel said it was in his mouth as honey for sweetness. Wow! What makes others cry if you obey, the Lord will become sweet for you? That's why in writing this book I'm not concerned with who doesn't see it, for some they will always reject Christ because they would rather follow their own views, or the opinions of others than the truth of the Word of God. But I'm going to give you the revelation: Jesus pre-existence can be found all throughout the Old Testament, and as He declares in John 8:58, *"Jesus said unto them, Verily, verily, I say unto you, Before Abraham was, I am."* I believe it, I see it in scripture, I understand that He has always existed and that He is God in the Torah, He is God from the prophets, and He is the Word that was made flesh in the New Testament.

"And the Word was made flesh, and dwelt among us, (and we beheld his glory, the glory as of the only begotten of the Father,) full of grace and truth." (John 1:14)

Chapter Seven
The Word came to Jonah

He didn't Run from his Call! He Ran from His face!
"Now the word of the LORD came unto Jonah the son of Amittai, saying, Arise, go to Nineveh, that great city, and cry against it; for their wickedness is come up before me. But Jonah rose up to flee unto Tarshish from the presence of the LORD, and went down to Joppa; and he found a ship going to Tarshish: so he paid the fare thereof, and went down into it, to go with them unto Tarshish from the presence of the LORD." (Jonah 1:1-3)

As a Pastor it's my desire to always make sure that the text is preached in its proper context. It's never good theology when we take scriptures out of their proper settings in order to prove a point or to have good preaching material. I find that many times we can all miss it concerning the Word of God. It's inerrant, but people are full of error, and often times we have good intentions. We are not butchering scripture on purpose, but sometimes God has to open up our eyes (like He did with his disciples on the road to Emmaus after his resurrection) so that we can see clearly what God meant when he said what he said. With that being said, Jonah was not running from his calling. He was not running from preaching. He was running from the God who had appeared unto him. He was running from the presence. I will prove this with the text.

"Now the word of the LORD came unto Jonah the son of Amittai, saying, Arise, go to Nineveh, that great city, and cry against it; for their wickedness is come up before me. But Jonah rose up to flee unto Tarshish from the presence of the LORD, and went down to Joppa; and he found a ship going t Tarshish: so he paid the fare thereof, and went down into it, to go with them unto Tarshish from the presence of the LORD." (Jonah 1:1-3)

Jonah thinks at this point, "Hold on! We don't even have a relationship. Who are you that's invading my space?

I don't know you!" We don't know how He appeared to
Jonah, but Jonah was terrified of the mere presence of the
Word. The Word presence gives us more clarity. From the
Hebrew it is the word "Paniym", and it means the face or
faces, the presence, or person. When the Word showed up
and Jonah saw His presence, His face, the Face of God it
terrified him to say the least. Jonah wasn't afraid to go and
preach to the people of Nineveh. I have heard some people
say that Jonah was racist and he wanted to keep the God of
the Jews Jewish. That's only a partial truth. Later in the
book of Jonah he shows disdain towards the people of
Nineveh, but that's not the reason he ran from God. Jonah
had an encounter with the Word and he was afraid of the
presence of God, the Face of God. He didn't know what to
do with the presence of God.

Think about it. If God just shows up in your room
and gives you all of these instructions and you have never
talked with Him before, you've never met Him before, you
have never been on assignment for him before, is it really
that easy to obey Him? I know some will say yes, but for
whatever reason, Jonah said no. In his wisdom he thought
he could out maneuver God, run away from God and go to
a place where God would not find him. That's the furthest
thing from the truth. Look at men in their folly running
from a God who is all seeing and all knowing.

*But Jonah rose up to flee unto Tarshish from the
presence of the LORD, and went down to Joppa; and he
found a ship going to Tarshish: so he paid the fare thereof,
and went down into it, to go with them unto Tarshish from
the presence of the LORD."*
Jonah would waste time, money, and energy in an effort to
escape the presence of God. He buys a boat ride to Tarshish
and brings the boat crew into his drama, all because he did
not want the presence of God, Who appeared unto him as
the Word of the Lord. You can't run or hide from the call
of God, that's true, but you can't run from his presence
either. When He wants to reveal himself to you and He

wants to use you, you have to be like Samuel and say, "Here I am God, speak, for your servant hears." You can't bring other people into your storm because you refuse to submit yourself to the will of God.

That's exactly what Jonah does. He acts like he can sleep the Lord's presence off like it's a bad dream, and he brings the whole shipping crew into his storm.

"But the LORD sent out a great wind into the sea, and there was a mighty tempest in the sea, so that the ship was like to be broken." (John 1:4)

God will use a storm in order to get you back on track. He will use tough times and hardships in your life in order to get you back into his perfect will. If God left up the entirety of our lives to us we would choose everything but Him. We will choose the night life over the Christ life and the clubs over the church. But, in his infinite wisdom, He knows how to create a storm that will shake everything in your life in order to get you back on track. The storm makes you have a face to face encounter with God. Let me say this, He knows how to make you cry 'uncle'.

When I was a kid there was a bully by the name of Joe. He was notorious in the neighborhood for making smaller kids cry 'uncle'. He would hunt you down and chase you to the front stairs of your house. Joe was a massive man in the eyes of elementary kids. Even though he was just a teenager, he looked grown and scary. Joe would catch you, place his two legs on top of your arms, and place so much pressure on you that you would scream "uncle". Then, having brought his victim into submission, he would get up and walk away. Well that may not be the best analogy, but you get the picture. God has a way of getting His servants and His sons in perfect alignment with His will, if they surrender.

"Then the mariners were afraid, and cried every man unto his god, and cast forth the wares that were in the ship into the sea, to lighten it of them. But Jonah was gone down

into the sides of the ship and he lay, and was fast
asleep. " (Jonah 1:5)
You can't sleep off the will of God. It's not a bad dream,
it's real—His presence, His power, His Word, and His call.
You can't get away with it because you close your
eyes or hide in the basement. God's presence will find you.
Look at the response of the ship master. He knows
something isn't right with this picture, and he says, "Hey,
you asleep! Get up and give me the real deal on what's
going on in my life, because whatever is after you is now
affecting my situation. Have you ever helped any one
whom God was spanking? I have and I'm here to tell you
it's the absolute worst feeling to be judged for helping
someone God is dealing with. I know many of us have a
savior complex and we try to play Jesus with most people
we meet but some people are in predicaments and under
judgment because God is dealing with them. It's not wise
to put your hands, your wisdom, and your life and
livelihood in position to be spanked when God extends His
right hand of justice upon them. It's like the little brother in
the way when his father is spanking his bigger brother. He
doesn't want to hurt you, but you got in the way and those
are the results that you'll get 10 out of 10 times.
"*So the shipmaster came to him, and said unto him,
What meanest thou, O sleeper? Arise, call upon thy God, if
so be that God will think upon us, that we perish not. And
they said everyone to his fellow, Come, and let us cast lots,
that we may know for whose cause this evil is upon us. So
they cast lots, and the lot fell upon Jonah. Then said they
unto him, tell us, we pray thee, for whose cause this evil is
upon us; what is thine occupation? And whence comest
thou? What is thy country? And of what people art thou?* "
(Jonah 1:6-8)
Even the worldly crew recognized that evil was upon them
based upon something someone else had done. They woke
up Jonah and they asked him to pray and ask God not to
allow them to perish. Jonah is in no rush to do that. He is

disconnected from God. He is unrighteous at the time and he doesn't want to be located by the Word of the Lord. God, however, never lost sight of him in the first place. So, they pull out there dice and they cast their lots. And Lo and behold, the lots fall on Jonah. They get a revelation that there's something different about this guy and they want to know what he does, where he's, from what's background, because God is moving all the sea in order to get to him. Look at Jonah's response

"And he said unto them, I am a Hebrew; and I fear the LORD, the God of heaven, which hath made the sea and the dry land." (Jonah 1:9)

Jonah gives the crew his pedigree. He talks about who he is, where he is from, and he explains to them why he got on their boat in the first place. This is the key to understanding that he wasn't running from the calling, he was running from the presence of God. He tells the men exactly why he got on the boat.

"Then were the men exceedingly afraid, and said unto him, Why hast thou done this? For the men knew that he fled from the presence of the LORD, because he had told them." (Jonah 1:10) He told them out of his own mouth why he got on their boat and brought havoc into their lives. It was because he was fleeing from the presence of the Lord. This is out of Jonahs mouth, recorded in the book of Jonah. *"For the men knew that he fled from the presence of the Lord because He told them."* The point I want to make in this scripture is that Jonah fled from the Word that appeared unto him. The beginning of chapter 1 states: *"Now the word of the LORD came unto Jonah the son of Amittai, saying . . ."* The Word came to Jonah "saying" and Jonah ran from the sight of the Word of the Lord. It wasn't until Jonah repented for his foolishness and got things right with God that the Word reappears and gives him the same instructions as before. Let us look at Jonah chapter 3:1. *"And the word of the LORD came unto Jonah the second*

time, saying . . . " Even though we blow it God always gives us a second chance.
    "Arise go unto Nineveh, that great city, and preach unto it the preaching that I bid thee. So Jonah arose, and went unto Nineveh, according to the word of the LORD. Now Nineveh was an exceeding great city of three days' journey. " (Jonah 3:2 -3)
    After studying the book of Jonah, I'm convinced that he ran from the Word that appeared to him, and like most believers who experience God's grace, we fall right back into the same traps that God had mercy on us and delivered from. Jonah forgets about the fact that he was just literally in hell. Whether it was in the fishes belly or in the lower parts of the earth, he was in the worst place of his life. Now that he was on dry ground he did what God asked him to do. He then caught an attitude (for whatever reason) about God being gracious to Nineveh, and like most believers who have an entitlement mentality, he missed the fact that God is God of the whole world, and not just their community church or clique. Jonah is rebuked in chapter 4 about having the wrong attitude towards plants instead of people. Sometimes we love the stuff (the missing coin the lost sheep) and we chase after that smiling. But, when it comes to our prodigal brother, we don't even want to look for them. Then, we find ourselves angry when they reappear and experience the grace of God, even though all along the only thing the Father wanted from the son was fellowship. In order to have fellowship with the Word you have to experience His presence and His appearing.

Chapter Eight
The Word made the Worlds!

"By the word of the LORD were the heavens made; and all the host of them by the breath of his mouth."(Psa. 33:6)
"In the beginning was the Word, and the Word was with God, and the Word was God. The same was in the beginning with God. All things were made by him; (the Word) and without him (the Word) was not anything made that was made." (John 1)
While the world gives credit to evolution for the creation of the planets, they debate who made what in there secular humanism. I've got a secret to share with all of humanity. Jesus, who was the Word, is the , and that very Word being God, created the world in which we know, see, and enjoy.
"God, who at sundry times and in divers manners spake in time past unto the fathers by the prophets, Hath in these last days spoken unto us by his Son, whom he hath appointed heir of all things, by whom also he made the worlds . . ." (Hebrews 11:1) He, the Son of God, the Word of God, the Word of the Lord, made, designed, built, and laid the foundations placed for our enjoyment and benefit. Consider the gold, silver diamonds, precious metals, minerals, oil reserves, and natural gas He made it. Let's look at Psalms 33:6, *"By the word of the LORD were the heavens made . . ."* the atmosphere we see and dwell in the heavens above and the galaxies we see (and those we cannot see) He created them. He was the one who said let there be light, and His Word is still traveling at the speed of light right now! He spoke the worlds into existence with his Word and the Bible says that everything that He made was good. I cannot exhaust the text with its unlimited revelation, but I can emphasize the superiority of the Word (Jesus) that has always existed from Genesis to Revelation. Jesus is more than Mary's Son.

He's more than the carpenter from Galilee. He is more than a prophet. He is more than *A* God as the Jehovah Witnesses call Him. He is *the* God that has appeared in this realm from the beginning. He created all things that we see and don't see. He is in charge of the Host of Heaven and all the host of them by the breath of his mouth. Let us revisit. Psalm 33:6. *"By the word of the LORD were the heavens made; and all the host of them by the breath of his mouth."* Jesus made every angel and every fallen angel, including Lucifer himself. He is in absolute control of principalities, powers, might, and dominions, yet he took on flesh and died on a cross for you and me. The bible says in Philippians 2:8, *"And being found in fashion as a man, he humbled himself, and became obedient unto death, even the death of the cross."* He was Found in Fashion as a man he unwrapped himself from his glory and splendor and he took on the suit or flesh of mankind to pay the price for all of our sins.

"And the Word was made flesh, and dwelt among us, (and we beheld his glory, the glory as of the only begotten of the Father,) full of grace and truth." (John 1: 14) I am amazed at His power. He can do anything. Is anything too hard for God? He asked Abraham in Genesis 18, but I am not just amazed by His power, I am amazed at what he became, a man with a man's name—Jesus. He put on his earth suit and kept it on so that the righteous One could take our filthy rags and give us new life that can only be found in the face of Jesus Christ.

"In the beginning was the Word, and the Word was with God, and the Word was God. The same was in the beginning with God. All things were made by him; (the Word) and without him (the Word) was not anything made that was made." (John 1: 1) He always existed. In Genesis He is the Word of the Lord that appears to Abram. Humanity calls Him Lord God. They call Him Jehovah. The angels who mediated the book call Him the Word of the Lord, for that is His name in Heaven. Read 1 John 5:7.

45

"For there are three that bear record in heaven, the Father, the Word, and the Holy Ghost: and these three are one." Look at His name in Heaven. They call Him the Word, Hallelujah, Glory to His Holy Name. While mankind is in search of solving all of the mysteries life has given them, all we need emphatically is the Word. In Closing the same God Who appeared to Abram and called him out of his father's house in Genesis 12:1, Who appeared to him as his protector and provider in Genesis 15:1, is the same God who appears on our behalf to His Father and takes His blood to the Mercy Seat, gives us access to the Holies of Holies, and makes God our Father. The Word says it like this (Jesus) talking with Mary after His resurrection (because death can never hold the Word) he says to Mary:

"Jesus saith unto her, Mary. She turned herself, and saith unto him, Rabboni; which is to say, Master. Jesus saith unto her, Touch me not; for I am not yet ascended to my Father: but go to my brethren, and say unto them, I ascend unto my Father, and your Father; and to my God, and your God." (John 20:16-17)

Hallelujah for access granted to our God and Father because of the finished work of Jesus Christ in His death, burial, and resurrection. He is Jesus, our soon coming King, the Word of the Lord, and the Word of truth.

"And I saw heaven opened, and behold a white horse; and he that sat upon him was called Faithful and True, and in righteousness he doth judge and make war. His eyes were as a flame of fire, and on his head were many crowns; and he had a name written, that no man knew, but he himself. 13And he was clothed with vesture dipped in blood: and his Name is called The Word of God." (Revelations 19: 11-13)

"Your father Abraham rejoiced to see my day: and he saw it, and was glad. Then said the Jews unto him, Thou art not yet fifty years old, and hast thou seen Abraham?

Jesus said unto them, Verily, verily I say unto you,
Before Abraham was, I am". (John 8:56-57)

Closing Notes

This is not an exhaustive study of how powerful the Word truly is its taking many easy to understand text and making them relevant so by two or three witnesses we can establish our principle truth. If you would study the Word of the Lord closely you will find many other examples of the appearing of The Word before he took on Flesh and kept it for you and for me. The points are very clear Jesus is The Word of the Lord who appeared in the Torah unto our Father Abraham. He appears to major and minor prophets throughout The Word of the Lord comes to Elijah in the Cave and He is that still small voice. It is the Word of the Lord that Buries Moses at his Death! And The Word becomes flesh to this day and dwells amongst us so that we can live. Jesus He is that Word, Who Was, Who Is, and Will always be God. Look at what the author and finisher of our faith tells the religious people of his day who was In Search of Eternal Life but not God

John 5:39 Search the scriptures; for in them ye think ye have eternal life: and they are they which testify of me. Jesus is having a conversation with The Jewish leaders of his time and he tells them yes you are reading and searching scriptures because you think In knowing scriptures it will give you eternal life He then makes it real plain what you see blurry right now testifies of me plainly, but you can't see me as The Word of God because you desire the Law of God but you don't desire a Relationship with The Word of God.

Which is greatest the book or the greatest Author?
In Psalms 82 the text states in v Psa 82:6 I have said, Ye *are* gods; and all of you *are* children of the most High. Notice what the Word says they are searching the book which testifies of him because is the author and finisher of our Faith. Psalms 82 V 6 I have said, Ye *are* gods; and all of you *are* children of the most High. The Word Says in the Old Testament I have said but look at what the Author of the book says to the reader of the book that's searching and looking for something that He created and said in John 10:33 The Jews answered him, saying, For a good work we stone thee not; but for blasphemy; and because that thou, being a man, makest thyself God.

John 10:34 Jesus answered them, Is it not written in your law, I said, Ye are gods?

Jesus is so much God he Declares what his Law said but they missed what the writer of the book wrote because they couldn't handle the package it came in Look at what Jesus says to the religious leaders of his day. John 10:34 Jesus answered them, Is it not written in your law, I said, Ye are gods? Notice the slight difference in Psa 82:6 I have said, Ye *are* gods; and all of you *are* children of the most High and John 10:34 Jesus answered them, Is it not written in your law, I said, Ye are gods?

In one verse he quoted what he had written as the Word I have said ye are Gods. In John 10 v 34 he says is it not written I said, ye are gods? Jesus makes it so clear. The Word said, I said ye are gods. The Word says, I am blessed, The Word says I am whole, The Word says I am delivered, The Word says I am Rich, The Word says right now we are once again made in the image and likeness of God. I said, the Word said it! Ye are gods! Thank you Lord for redemption that can only be found in the Face of Jesus Christ. And his Name Shall be Called the Word of God!!!

Made in the USA
Monee, IL
12 June 2023

35533394R10030